A New Way to Buy a Car

How to Put Yourself in the "Driver's Seat" by Navigating the Process Like a Pro

Gordon Wright, MBA

Copyright © 2015 Nevco Marketing

All rights reserved.

ISBN: 978-0-9940390-0-2

DEDICATION

Dear Car Buyer/Shopper;
Choosing a new or used vehicle isn't easy. Why? Because you're bombarded with misleading advertising, confusing terminology, barely-competent sales people, and simply bad information from high-pressure sales to near-worthless decision-making methods. How do you even find a qualified, competent professional car dealership or salesperson? **You start by reading this consumer guide**. In this fact-filled book based on my years of experience working in the car business, you'll <u>discover how to avoid the pitfalls</u> that trip up novice <u>and</u> experienced buyers alike. In this guide, you will discover:

- Four Steps to a Hassle-Free Car Purchase
- Six Costly Misconceptions About Buying a Car
- Four Car Sales Rip-Offs to Avoid
- Ten Mistakes to Avoid When Visiting a Dealership

After over seven years in the car business, I realized that knowledgeable and informed buyers are the easiest to work with and are more willing to get right to the point and appreciate a relationship that is based on mutual respect. So, I wrote this guide to help you better understand car buying. Now, with this information, you can make an informed, intelligent decision and avoid the most common pitfalls. And, if you have any questions about car buying or how dealerships operate, you're invited to contact me at www.AFriendintheCarBusiness.com. I have dedicated my business to educating consumers. I'll be happy to help in every way I can.

Cordially,
Gordon Wright,
Your Friend in the Car Business
www.AFriendintheCarBusiness.com

CONTENTS

	Acknowledgments	i
1	Four Steps to a Hassle-Free Car Purchase	1
2	Six Costly Misconceptions About Buying a Car	7
3	Four Car Sales Rip-Offs to Avoid	16
4	Ten Mistakes to Avoid When Visiting a Dealership	20
5	A Few Other Important Matters to Consider	33
6	What Fees Must You Pay on a New Car?	42
7	Why You Want a Friend in the Car Business	45
8	RESOURCES	46

ACKNOWLEDGMENTS

Thanks to the increasing number of car sales professionals who are not pressured by "old school" sales managers into employing the tactics and manipulations that this book is meant to overcome. This small but growing number of sales people gives me the hope and inspiration that the retail car business will continue to move into the 21st Century and leave the methods of the past behind. Until that becomes the situation across the industry, consumers must continue to be alert and ready to deal with the minority of bad apples still plying their trade at dealerships across the country.

This book will help you find those enlightened sales people who are dedicated to serving customers in an open and transparent fashion and it will also help you to spot and deal with those who are still working with attitudes and approaches from an earlier century. Buying a car should be fun and can be an enjoyable experience if you keep your wits about you and use the information in this book to locate car sales professionals who are interested in creating customers for life.

1 FOUR STEPS TO A HASSLE-FREE CAR PURCHASE

It really is possible to turn a potentially scary and frustrating endeavor into an easy and pleasant experience as long as you follow the advice in this guide. Car dealerships and car salespeople want the process to go smoothly as well, however, this is most likely to happen when the car purchaser (i.e., you) is familiar with how the process works and approaches the project with knowledge and confidence. This guide will help you do that. Let's get started…

Step #1

Know What You Want/Need

Separating what you need from what you want can be the most difficult part of the car buying experience but if you do not have these two issues clear in your head before you head out to the Auto Mall, you are likely to become frustrated and/or taken advantage of by shrewd car sales people.

Here's an exercise to help you sort out what kind of vehicle makes the most sense given your current transportation situation and future plans. Answer the questions and then check the recommendations:

a. **How many people will be in the car most of the time?** If, for 90% of the time and mileage, it is only you and possibly one other person in the car, then a small, fuel-efficient car may be all you need and a sub-compact or compact car will fit the bill. If you expect half a dozen out-of-town family or friends to visit from time to time, consider renting a van for those weekends rather than buying a bigger car that you don't really need on a daily basis. Even most sub-compact cars will seat four people comfortably. (If you are above average in height and/or weight, the sub-compact option may not work for you). Of course, if you are <u>frequently</u> transporting several people and/or cargo, a family-size sedan, Sport Utility Vehicle (SUV), or mini-van might better suit your requirements.

b. **What kind of activities will the vehicle be required to address?** For example, if you are an outdoor enthusiast who is headed to the ski hills every weekend during the winter, you may decide that All-Wheel-Drive would be worth having on your next vehicle to handle that deep snow or the unpredictable weather you will frequently encounter. If it's mainly a commuter car, the comments about the number of people normally in the car will give you the answer. If you are a home improvement enthusiast, those trips to Home Depot for 2x4's and wood panels will go a lot better with a van or SUV or even a truck. And for young families with kids, a mini-van is hard to beat when you need to be getting your kids and a few of the neighbors' kids to the soccer game or hockey rink (along with their equipment). Make sure that the new vehicle lines up with your lifestyle and fits within an overall transportation plan.

c. **Does the vehicle mix in your driveway make sense?** If you have (or need) two or more vehicles to accommodate the number of drivers in the family, think about what combination of vehicle types will provide the best mix. One large family vehicle and one small commuter vehicle might be the optimum way to cover the number-of-people-normally-in-the-car issue as well as the kinds-of-activities for which the vehicles will be needed. Also, the age and life expectancy of the vehicles in the driveway will help determine which vehicle is now the one to be replaced and what kind of vehicle/driver re-assignment would make the most sense. There is no right or wrong answer, however, these should be among your considerations.

d. **What makes sense for your family lifecycle stage?** Every five to seven years, you will find that the family needs change as kids grow and leave home and your transportation needs (or wants) change. Have a plan that sees you rotating your "fleet" of vehicles so the mini-van makes way for other transportation as the kids grow and move out. Plus you do not want all the vehicles in your driveway aging and coming due for replacement at the same time. If you can replace vehicles before they lose all their value, you will also lower maintenance costs and put yourself in a position to get that two-seater sports car before you are too old to enjoy it.

Step #2
Know What You Can Afford

Before you head to your local car dealership with that newspaper ad that shouts out that you can own that shiny new (insert your favorite car brand) for as little as $199 a month, take a step back and think of all the costs involved in car ownership (particularly if this is your first car). Also, those ads that make just about any car appear affordable are usually talking about a base-level vehicle and/or are assuming a hefty down payment which you might not have available.

The CAA has a handy calculator online at http://caa.ca/car_costs/ that highlights costs (including depreciation). This is a bit academic but works if you are paying cash for the car. If you are financing or leasing the car, you are probably most interested in how the new car impacts your cash flow. In a finance or lease scenario, you will have car payments plus insurance premiums, and gas and maintenance costs (although the latter will be minimal during the first few years when you are covered by the manufacturer's comprehensive warranty).

To get a ballpark figure for the monthly payment you can afford, **Consumer Reports** recommends that your total debt payment be no more than 36 percent of your gross income. Going by this rule, you can use the following steps to calculate how much of your monthly income you can comfortably afford to put toward your auto payments:
- Calculate 36 percent of your gross monthly income.
- Total all your monthly payments, including your mortgage or rent, credit card bills, and other instalment loans.
- Subtract the total of all your monthly payments from the 36 percent figure.

For example, if your pre-tax income is $75,000, total debt payments should not exceed $27,000 a year (36% of $75,000). If your existing debt payments equal, say, $20,000 a year, you can afford to pay $7,000 annually, or $583 a month, for car payments.

Step #3
Find a Dealer You Can Trust

Despite the sophisticated information technology now available to put the buyer in the driver's seat (excuse the pun), buying a car is still a major decision with a big emotional component. Plus, to complete the vehicle selection and find the right financing package means you are going to be visiting the dealership and interacting with a car salesperson. (A lot of people find that, alone, a scary prospect and that's why I will recommend, later in this book, that you deal with the Internet Manager or Sales Manager). It is becoming easier to do the entire process via phone and email so you can avoid coming into the dealership for anything other than signing the final purchase documents. However, this only works for a segment of the population who have bought many vehicles and know exactly what they want. For most shoppers, it will not guarantee that you get the right car.

The truth is that, with the odd exception, most people end up making a final decision on which car to buy and how they are going to pay for it when they are at the dealership and have found a salesperson who is helpful and trustworthy. But this doesn't mean you can't use the internet to make the process easier and less stressful. With the internet, you can "audition" your prospective salesperson before you go to the dealership.

Some internet shoppers seem to overlook the opportunity to use this medium to seek out a competent and professional salesperson and, instead, use the net to try and negotiate a final price via email. This simply encourages the less than professional sales people out there to use various tricks to get you into the dealership. Use the internet and the phone to find a person you can trust.

At most dealerships, internet inquiries are handled by a senior salesperson or by the sales manager. Once you receive a reply to your internet or email query, find out if this is someone you want to do business with. When you send in a quote/information request, you should get a very prompt response. Many people send requests to multiple dealers in their area. Here's your chance to gauge the responses. Who was quickest to respond? Who provided a bit more information or a few alternative suggestions? Who sent you a personalized response versus an automated response? If you provided a phone number, you should expect a call. Are you getting straight answers to your questions or are you finding the dealership person to be evasive?

Because almost nobody buys a car over the phone or internet, dealership sales people will want you to visit the dealership. Use your email and phone conversations to determine who is the most deserving of your business before making an appointment. Once you feel you have someone at the other end of the line who is committed to helping you, book an appointment and arrive armed with the questions that you are most keen to have answered and an idea of what features the "perfect vehicle" will have. If you have multiple vehicles in your household or you are "upside down" on a lease that you need to get out of, let the salesperson know your situation and ask for alternatives for you to consider.

Sometimes, new technology just makes life more complicated. Use the power of the internet to simplify the car buying process and get connected to a car salesperson who will act as your adviser instead an adversary. Find a friend and enjoy the car buying process as much as you plan to enjoy your new car.

Step #4
Read and Understand the Purchase Agreement
If you purchase a new or used vehicle, you will need to sign a Vehicle Purchase Agreement to make the deal binding. Despite the fact that the following notice is provided in **bold type** right above the purchaser's signature on all contracts signed in Ontario, <u>many car buyers sign without fully understanding the commitment they are making</u>. Here is what the note says and what you are agreeing to when you sign the agreement:

ALL SALES FINAL. Please review the entire Agreement, including all attached statements, before signing. This Agreement is final and binding once you have signed it unless the motor vehicle dealer has failed to comply with certain legal obligations.

First, in Ontario, there is no "cooling off" period when purchasing a motor vehicle. If you want to cancel a vehicle purchase agreement, the dealer is entitled to claim "liquidated damages" and retain a part – or all – of your deposit. In practice, most dealerships will make every effort to accommodate reasonable requests from buyers even after the deal is done, however, there is no legal obligation to do so. Some of the obvious things you should check before signing involve the vehicle you are purchasing and the accessories and add-ons included in the deal:

- <u>Are all the accessories you ordered clearly showing</u>? If the salesperson mentioned throwing in free oil changes for a year or an iPod to close the deal, make sure they are listed on the agreement, otherwise, everyone's memory will become suddenly cloudy when you come to pick up the car and ask about those extras.
- <u>Is the model code showing and color code indicated</u>? It doesn't happen often, but it is not uncommon for a customer to "think" they were buying a specific trim level but a different trim level and/or color was put on the agreement. When this happens, (in my experience) it's seldom malicious, however mistakes happen. If you ordered a vehicle with that technology package, make sure it appears on the agreement.
- <u>Are you paying for things you never discussed</u>? If you find

administration fees or other charges you don't understand, be sure you get an explanation before you sign. This is a favorite area to bury extra charges with the hope that you don't notice.

Don't Forget to Read the Back

On the back of the agreement are several statements that you are also agreeing to comply with. For example, the dealer has 90 days to deliver your car. No matter what the salesperson said about it only taking a week or two to get the car for you, the dealership can delay delivery for a number of reasons. (Or, they may have trouble getting the exact trim/color you ordered in a timely fashion). Unless it is written into the agreement, there is no obligation by dealer to provide you with a loaner car or free rental if your vehicle is delayed for any reason. I have seen vehicles delayed for lots of reasons including labor stoppages at the port, difficulty getting another dealer to transfer a vehicle, transportation companies "misplacing" the vehicle in transit, to name a few. Believe me, the dealer wants to deliver a sold vehicle as quickly as possible because no one at the dealership gets paid until the vehicle is delivered.

Trade-in Disclosures

The Ontario Motor Vehicle Act requires that the seller of any used car completely disclose all relevant information on the vehicle being sold. If you have a trade-in, you are selling your old car to the dealership. If you fail to disclose a material fact about your old car, you are liable to future owners of that vehicle. That's why the dealer taking in your trade, will ask you to sign a series of disclosures about your trade-in. Be sure to declare all relevant facts (such as previous damage exceeding $3,000, etc.) before handing over your trade-in.

One Last Comment

I have seen lots of people shopping for a new car traveling from dealer to dealer while considering several makes/models before working out a final deal at a dealership. The danger in "over shopping" is that when you finally decide on a vehicle, you may have assumed something in the deal that was part of a discussion at another dealership. Or, you test drove a GT model and ended up settling for a GS model (which is missing a couple of features important to you). Because I have seen this happen, I recommend reviewing the "fine print" before signing and before making the final commitment.

2 SIX COSTLY MISCONCEPTIONS ABOUT BUYING A CAR

Misconception #1
The Best Deals are Only Available at Certain Times

If asked, "When is the best time to buy a new car?", most people would probably answer the question by saying **"the end of the model year"** for the vehicle you have in mind. The rationale, of course, is that no manufacturer or dealer wants to have the old model year inventory once the new vehicles have arrived and they are willing to cut a deal to clear the remaining prior model year vehicles. That's normally what I tell customers as well, however, <u>when is</u> the end of the model year? It turns out that any month could be the end of the model year. In the "old days", September was the month that the new models arrived (especially on American car dealers' lots). And that is probably why August is still the highest sales month for most dealerships. But now, with production cycles staggered to minimize downtime and cars being shipped from Europe, Japan, and all over North America, new models may start arriving as early as July and as late as December. And, if the new model year vehicle has undergone a major styling update, manufacturers are now frequently launching the new vehicles during <u>the first</u> quarter (January through March).

When you buy at the end of the model year, you are often foregoing the opportunity to get the latest technology that is coming on the new vehicle. For example, all 2011 model year vehicles were required to include <u>electronic stability control</u>, which was not available (and not required) on all vehicles in 2010. If you saved some money on your 2010 model year purchase, you may find that the trade-in value in 4 or 5 years is lower if you missed getting this important safety feature.

With a struggling economy and a more competitive marketplace, car manufacturers have had to become smarter about matching supply and demand. Rather than building cars "just in case" customers came in to buy, the new paradigm is to build the cars "just in time". This means that during the model year, manufacturers are monitoring the inventory in the pipeline on a monthly basis and adjusting production, promotions, and incentives (specifically by model). The objective is to be selling the last few vehicles from the current model year when the new model year vehicles start to arrive. The manufacturers and their dealers are getting very good at this balancing act. The system is not perfect but <u>the truth about model year clearance events</u> is that you can usually get a deal but it often is not on the color or trim level that you want. And, I have seen customers deciding to wait for a few more weeks to get a better deal only to find that the model they want is sold out when they come back.

If you have your eye on a particular brand/model and you have the flexibility to wait for the end of the model year, make sure you do the following to maximize your savings:

- ***Find out when the new model year vehicles are starting to arrive***. This is normally the point where both the <u>selection</u> and the <u>incentives</u> are at or near their max. You can find out by simply calling your local dealership and saying you are interested in the new model year vehicles and ask when they will start arriving. That's the point at which you will want to check out the remaining inventory and yearend incentives on the outgoing model year vehicles.
- ***Do the final deal near the end of the month***. High volume dealers that are trying to hit volume targets for that month are often more willing to cut a real deal just to hit a volume target and if you schedule the delivery for early the following month, you may be able to get the dealer to "protect" the deal in case the manufacturer boosts the incentives for the following month.
- ***Consider paying cash***. Sometimes, the cash incentives are better than the finance incentives. Also, your best payment on a specific car may be found by negotiating the cash price and financing the car at the preferred dealership finance rate. Consider both options before buying.

Misconception #2
You Can Save Money by Paying Cash
In recent years, the use of low financing rates by auto manufacturers as

A NEW WAY TO BUY A CAR

an incentive to purchase a new car has "progressed" to the point where there is an expectation that 0% financing will be available on any and all vehicles in the dealer's showroom. I have even had customers come into the store and ask if we had 0% financing (before finding out if we had the type of vehicle that might fit their needs). Because everyone has now been conditioned to accept nothing other than 0% financing, they are often missing an opportunity to save money.

Toward the end of the model year for a vehicle, the 0% financing incentives often get extended to 60 or 72 months so that the outgoing model year vehicles get moved off the lot as the new model year vehicles arrive. The car manufacturers use their marketing funds to buy down the finance rates to these very attractive levels. When you buy a car under these 0% terms, you normally forego the option to pay cash (which may mean passing up a significant rebate or discount off the price). With a cash purchase, the car manufacturer "saves" the marketing funds that would have been used to reduce the rate to 0% and provides a **cash rebate/discount**. But, did you know that you can take the cash discount and still finance the car.

With most car brands, you can take the "discount for cash" and still finance the vehicle at the standard rate (which is the preferred rate that the manufacturer has negotiated with the bank). For example, right now, you can buy an outgoing model year **Mazda5** and finance it for 60 months at 0% **OR** you can take the $4,500 cash discount and finance it at 4.99% for the same period. Which option would you choose? Check out the table below:

Purchase Options	0% Option	Cash w/4.99%
Vehicle MSRP*	$23,195	$23,195
Freight, PDI**, Fees	$2,025	$2,025
Mfgr. Discount for Cash	$0	($4,500)
Cost of the Car	$25,220	$20,720
Sales Tax at 13%	$2,694	$3,279
Amount to Finance	$28,499	$23,414
Cost of Financing	$0	$3,090
Total Amount Paid	$28,499	$26,504
Monthly Payment	$475	$442

*MSRP = Manufacturer's Suggested Retail Price
**PDI or PDE = Pre-Delivery Inspection or Pre-Delivery Expense

It turns out you save $1,995 over 60 months if you choose the Cash Discount option. So, you are not saving money (in this case) by opting for the 0% financing. You are paying more! And, another benefit, if you pay off the loan early, you save some of the interest that is not possible on the 0% option.

Effectively, there are two prices for this car. You need to calculate which program works best for you. Depending on the "standard finance rate" and the amount of the "discount for cash" on the vehicle you are considering, it may be to your advantage to opt for the Cash Purchase option even though you are not financing it at 0%.

Misconception #3
Asking Several Dealers for Their "Best Price" Gets the Best Deal

Many, if not most, car buyers now use the internet to do preliminary research when considering a car purchase, which is great because an informed buyer is a better buyer. Even most car salespeople would agree with this statement. However, some car buyers then decide on a specific make/model and use the internet to get competing dealers to bid on the selected vehicle. This car shopping approach seems simple and logical but it can complicate the process as well as lead to disappointment and I'll tell you why.

If it were not for something called Human Nature, getting several Honda dealers in your area to bid on supplying you with a specific Civic (substitute the make/model of your choice) would seem to be a simple way to get the best price. What could go wrong? Every dealer is just going to provide their best price and hope you choose them, right? Not quite!

If you ask competing dealers to bid on supplying a specific car, they all want to get the business and they all want to do it at a profit (or at worst, breakeven). Now, leaving the possibility of outright dishonesty aside, every bidding dealer has an incentive (in this situation) to structure the bid so it **appears** to be the lowest. They can do this by:
- Quoting a "cash purchase" price instead of a low interest finance price
- Leaving out certain fees, taxes, and levies
- Assuming in the quote that certain fees will be paid upfront and only the balance is used to calculate the monthly finance payment
- Quoting a payment based on a longer term than requested
- Quoting on a slightly different version of the vehicle than requested (or understood)
- Assuming some rebates for which you may not qualify (e.g. first time buyer, student, loyalty program, etc.)

So, you send out your request for quotation to several Honda dealers (to stay with the example above) and you get back various different numbers and different levels of detail. If all the dealers are acting ethically and your specifications are very detailed, *there should not be more than a couple of hundred dollars difference between the highest quote and the lowest quote.* Now what do you do? In the final analysis, this is likely to be the case if every dealer is quoting on the same assumptions because dealer margins on popular car makes/models are only 6% to 8%. Go to CarCostCanada.com or UnHaggle.com if you want verification (or TrueCar.com in the US). (This is the best way I know to quickly determine the best available price that any dealership should be willing to provide).

A more likely scenario is that you will get one or two quotes that appear to be a couple of thousand dollars lower than the rest. Now what do you do? Clearly, two dealers selling the same car under the same terms in an extremely competitive market cannot be off by a few thousand dollars. The only explanation is that the low-ball bidder (and usually that's just what it is) has provided a **phony number** (using one of the above assumptions) in order to get you into the dealership. If you get a bid like this, it is a red flag that something fishy is going on.

All dealers in Ontario know that you can only legally purchase a motor vehicle by presenting yourself at the dealership and signing a purchase agreement on the premises. Therefore, dealers will do their utmost to get you in the store with the assumption that they can close the sale on terms that favor the dealership. That's why it is a recipe for confusion and frustration to send out requests for quotation when there are other means available to determine a fair price without going through a blizzard of back and forth emails to numerous dealerships to "clarify" the bids and still not be sure once you select a "winning bidder".

Misconception #4
Aggressive Negotiating Will Get You the Best Deal

I always suggest that car buyers Negotiate After Buying the Car! I know that sounds illogical at first glance, but hear me out. Often, customers (mistakenly) spend a lot of time and emotional energy negotiating a discount on the price of the vehicle only to over pay for protection packages and other add-ons (such as tinted windows, rustproofing, accessories, etc.) when they are signing the paperwork in the business office. It is my contention that you are actually better off to pay the sticker price on the car and then negotiate on the extras (many of which are worth having and help to hold the value of the car but are usually over-priced).

Now there is nothing wrong with negotiating with the dealer to save some money on the price of the car. But, most customers who are set on saving money on their purchase (or fear that they will be ripped off if they don't play hard ball) are so satisfied with themselves after hammering the dealer for a significant discount that they <u>let down their defenses</u> when they sit down with the business manager. That's where the dealer makes most of the profit on the overall sale. Now that you "own" the car and you have saved money on the purchase, you are more <u>susceptible to a skillful sales pitch</u> on protecting your investment with rust proofing, additional warranty protection, or other add-ons (often at inflated prices).

The car business is not unlike other big ticket retail products in that the margin that the retailer makes on a flat screen TV or SLR camera is small compared to what they make on the camera case or added warranty package. <u>Edmunds.com</u> (USA data) recently listed the gross margin on the most popular compact cars:

Toyota Corolla	6.5%
Ford Focus	5.5%
Honda Civic	7.8%
Hyundai Elantra	2.7%
Mazda3	6.2%

If you consider that Walmart (the king of discount retailing) makes an average gross margin of 25% and Costco makes about 15%, the margins being made on popularly priced new cars are pretty thin. Consider also that there are over 25 compact car brands competing for the available business so there is not much room for car companies to hide thousands of dollars of margin and still be competitive. For cars that are built outside North America, it is even tougher as these cars must pay the 6.1% non-NAFTA tariff and still price themselves against locally built vehicles.

You might ask, how can dealerships survive on these thin margins? The answer is, they don't. Dealerships make their money on used cars, the service and parts department, and the additional products and services you buy once you have committed to purchase your new car, i.e., rust protection packages, extended warranties, tinted windows, dealer installed accessories, and other add-ons. Dealers also get rebates from the manufacturer for hitting volume targets and achieving customer service targets at the end of the year.

Most dealers will agree to sell their new vehicles at 3% to 4% above dealer cost which you can get by subscribing to CarCostCanada.com or Unhaggle.com (or TrueCar.com in the U.S.) where you can obtain the dealer's invoice cost on any vehicle including any incentives or rebates currently on the car. Or, save yourself the $39.95 and ask your dealer to show you the factory invoice for the car you are purchasing. Most dealerships do not have a problem showing you the invoice if you are ready to buy the car. If they refuse, find another dealer. But save the hard bargaining for the business office where their aim is to recover whatever was lost up front and then some.

Misconception #5
Using Your Line-of-Credit is a Good Idea

There are a lot of prudent ways to use a Line-of-Credit but using it to buy a car is probably not one of them. One of the dangers of putting an automobile on a Line-of-Credit is that if you miss a payment, the bank can simply deduct the money from your savings or chequing account. Or, in a worst-case scenario, foreclose on your house if it is a Home Equity Line-of-Credit.

But a more rational reason for not using a Line-of-Credit is the unstructured nature of the loan. It's what I call the "Never Never Loan" because it never seems to get paid off. Once you have put a few purchases on your Line-of-Credit, you start to lose track of whether the car is anywhere near being paid off. With a proper car loan, you know where you are at any point and you will eventually get it paid off. If you miss payments on a structured car loan, the worst that can happen is that the car gets re-possessed (not your home).

Some people are tempted to use their Line-of-Credit because the ***variable rate*** they are getting is lower than the ***fixed rate*** available through the dealer (particularly on used cars). But a variable rate is just that...variable. Therefore, a fixed rate that is guaranteed for the full term of the loan and is fully open (to be paid off without penalty) is the preferred method of financing your new or used car.

If you are buying a used car that's less that five years old, the car loan you get through the dealer will likely be better than what your bank can provide to you directly. That's because the major banks have a huge dealer lending program that sees rates that can be as low as 3.9% to 6.9%. On older cars (and for weaker borrowers), rates are double or triple these levels. Right now, because pre-owned vehicles are a stronger focus at most dealerships, car manufacturers and financial institutions have come up with much sharper pricing of rates for used cars than in the past. But if you are quoted a finance rate on a used car by your dealer, remember, **the rate is negotiable** if your credit is good. Also remember that loans under $10,000 carry the highest rates.

If you are buying a <u>new car</u>, very low (or 0%) finance rates are available for credit worthy buyers. These rates are subsidized by the car manufacturer to help the dealership sell cars. You may find that the rates are so low on a new car purchase that the monthly payments for a new car are very similar to those for a used car because the interest cost difference is greater than the list price difference. That's why it usually makes sense to pay cash for a used car (if you have the cash) but finance a new car.

Misconception #6
Selling Your Current Vehicle Yourself is Better Than Trading In

When it comes time to retire your vehicle, you have a decision to make regarding what to do with the old car that is no longer meeting your needs. <u>You essentially have 4 choices</u>: You can **KEEP IT, GIVE IT AWAY, SELL IT YOURSELF, or SELL IT TO THE DEALER.**

You may have your own reasons for keeping it or giving it away. As a Car Sales Professional, I cannot help with those two options except to advise you in general terms. Now the question is: **Are you planning to sell it yourself or sell it to the dealer?**

If You Sell It Yourself, You Need Two Things: <u>Time & Money</u>

You Also Need to:
- Find Parking Space
- Keep it Insured
- Clean & Detail It
- Re-condition It (Repair what is not working)
- Advertise It
- Show It (including Booking Appointments & Road Tests)
- Get an M.T.O. Used Car Package (in Ontario)
- Provide a Bill of Sale
- Provide a CarProof (or CarFax) Vehicle History Report
- Collect Cash/Certified Funds

- Forego the Sales Tax Benefit

If You Sell It To The Dealer: <u>**You Enjoy these Benefits and Avoid some Risks**</u>
- The Dealer Pays Fair Value for your "<u>As Is</u>" Condition Vehicle
- The Dealer takes on the Time and Risk of Selling Your Vehicle
- You Simply Drop off Your Old Vehicle and Drive Away in Your New Vehicle.

The popular belief is that you can get more money by putting a "for sale" sign on your car or paying for online advertising and selling it yourself than if you trade it in at a dealer. Many people hold that belief because they see values for similar vehicles online that are higher than what the dealer is offering.

Most dealers should be able to get you the Black Book (wholesale) price for your "as is" vehicle which will be lower than the <u>retail asking prices</u> you will find on Autotrader and similar sites. Typically, prices appearing online from private sellers and dealerships are not the prices that the vehicles eventually sell at. As well, dealers selling used cars are normally including some safety certification, warranty, and special financing.

A frequent scenario that I have run into with trade-in vehicles is a customer who has a trade-in offer from me (the dealership) and has a buyer (more or less lined up) who is willing to pay more but wants the vehicle safety certified. During the safety certification process, the mechanic discovers a mechanical problem that must be repaired. Once all the costs of getting the vehicle certified are calculated, there is often very little difference from the offer received from the dealer.

I always suggest to customers that if they are in such a quandary, they can go with the **<u>firm offer from the dealer</u>** (as their fall back position) and continue to try and sell their trade-in vehicle until it is time to take delivery of their new car. If they do better privately in the meantime, they can pocket the difference. It's a win/win.

3 FOUR CAR SALES RIP-OFFS TO AVOID

Rip-Off #1
Rustproofing

As someone who has personally purchased rustproofing on most of the vehicles I have ever owned, I am not suggesting that you not buy rustproofing for your new car, however, <u>paying too much for rustproofing is where the rip-off usually occurs</u>. As I explain elsewhere in this guide, you should be prepared to <u>negotiate</u> on any after-purchase products and services but you need to know what is reasonable.

Once you have purchased the vehicle and you are sitting in the Business Manager's office getting the final paperwork completed and banking arrangements sorted out, you will be offered the opportunity to "<u>protect</u>" your vehicle by getting one or more of the following done: rustproofing, undercoating, fabric protection, and paint protection. Often, these are packaged together. Usually these extras are sold as "just two or three more dollars on your biweekly payment". Find out what the total amount will be and ask yourself if it makes sense. Dealers often get away with selling these packages for thousands of dollars when you really should be paying hundreds.

The two rust protection methods available are <u>Spray Protection</u> and <u>Electronic Module Protection</u>. Here's how they compare and work:
1. **Spray**. Best done when the car is new, this approach involves spraying various substances on the underside of the vehicle as well as inside rocker panels, the hood, trunk, doors and wheel wells to coat surfaces to prevent moisture and road chemicals, such as salt, from interacting with the metal. These are three basic methods:

a. <u>Oil-Based</u> is applied annually and is good at working its way into the many crevices where rust can potentially get started. The major provider of this treatment is **Krown**. This is the method recommended by the **Automobile Protection Association**. Oil-based products have a tendency to drip for several days after application and must be re-applied to maintain the protective affect.
   b. <u>Silicone Based</u> products are most commonly **offered by car dealerships**. They are colorless and exhibit a waxy texture that eventually solidifies. They require only one application and do not drip but will only be effective if applied liberally by a well-trained and conscientious technician.
   c. <u>Tar Based</u> approach is otherwise known as **undercoating**. It involves spraying a black, tar-like substance on the exposed parts of the under body of your car, which then solidifies and acts as a permanent shield against moisture, salt, and other chemicals. The major risk to tar-based solutions is that if not applied properly and thoroughly, cracks may develop in the coating over time and trap moisture within itself, leading to rust. Ziebart is one of the largest providers of this method of rust protection and charges approximately $150 per vehicle.
2. **Electronic Module**. The favorite product for dealers to sell is an Electronic Module which involves installing a small device in your car that then sends a weak electric current through the metal and in theory stops it from rusting. The **Automobile Protection Association**'s website currently states "the APA is not convinced that electronic anti-rust devices provide good protection compared to the available alternatives. We do not recommend them." If you want this technology, CounterAct Electronic Rust Protection System is sold by Canadian Tire for $299 plus installation.

There is considerable debate regarding whether you should get rustproofing and lots of opinions as to which method is best. According to <u>Consumer Reports,</u> in their annual auto survey, "Today's vehicles are manufactured with good corrosion protection … rust problems have almost vanished in modern vehicles." Ask about the car manufacturer's Rust Perforation Warranty. Most standard rust-through warranties for domestic and imported vehicles now run five years or more. **If you decide to get rustproofing on your vehicle (and decide to do it at the dealership), understand what it is costing and do not accept the first offer!**

Rip-Off #2
"Police Traceable" Etching

Most car dealers (new and used) try to charge additional fees to increase the profit on the car. The fees will have names such as Doc Fees, Admin Fees, Security Package, Security Etching, Nitrogen, Road Hazard Protection, Key Fob Protection, and lots of others. Your first duty is to <u>make sure all charges are explained</u> and ask yourself if they make sense. Then, negotiate them off the deal or reduce the cost being quoted. If the dealer cannot <u>explain the benefit</u> provided by each and why it is worth what they are charging, have it removed or reduced. Some of the benefits are nice to have but the dealer's cost to provide these protections is low so there is usually room to negotiate the fees lower. Generally, dealers over-charge for these extras.

Rip-Off #3
Life & Other Insurance

Here is another area where the dealership can often take advantage of an unprepared car buyer and offer <u>a good product at an inflated price</u>. There is a great case to be made for protecting yourself against a situation where you cannot make the finance payments on your car. Those might include <u>losing your job</u>, short term or long term <u>disability</u>, catastrophic <u>illness</u>, or <u>death</u>. Once you have decided to purchase the vehicle, the Financial Services Manager (also called the Business Manager or Finance & Insurance Manager) will likely offer you the opportunity to protect yourself from Loss of Employment, Personal Injury or Disability, or Death by adding insurance policies that will provide the funds necessary to pay off the car loan and/or provide monthly income (in the case of employment loss or disability) to cover your car payments.

There are two issues here: <u>First</u>, you can usually ***purchase the same coverage at your bank or insurance company that you already do business with at a <u>fraction of the cost</u>*** and <u>Second</u>, the policies you buy at the dealership will be underwritten by ***an insurer who may or may not be in business*** when and if you have to make a claim. (In a worse case scenario, the dealership may be issuing the policy which would make it even riskier that you might not be able to collect). For example, if you are financing a $25,000 car purchase over 5 years, my recommendation would be to consider getting a <u>five-year term life insurance policy</u> for $25,000 from a reputable financial institution of your choice plus <u>private disability insurance</u> for the same period. It is likely that you can do it at less than half the cost of buying this at the dealership and with less risk. Your bank or car insurance company is the first place to go to get a quote and find out what you will need.

Rip-Off #4
Demo Vehicles

Most new car dealerships have <u>demonstrator vehicles</u> that are used for test drives by prospective customers. These vehicles usually cover a cross section of the brand product line and are driven by the management and sales team. At a typical dealership, each team member uses the demo for personal use and makes sure the vehicle is available for test drives during business hours. These cars usually go on the road for up to 15,000 kilometers and, prior to that point, they are taken off the road and sold at a discount as demonstrator vehicles. These vehicles normally still qualify as "new cars" (if they are under 15,000 kilometers) so they are still eligible for the new car incentives available from the factory. Because demos are normally discounted to clear them off the lot, you can save money by buying a demo, however, consider the following if you are considering a demo;

- You will lose some of the new car warranty that you would normally get (i.e., if the car has 10,000 km on it, you will lose that from the mileage allowance).
- The discount may not be enough to offset the mileage and wear and tear that you are agreeing to accept.
- Only if you are lucky, you will find that the demo that is available perfectly matches the trim level, package and color that you wanted. Most often, it will be a compromise or you will be paying the same amount (as you would for the new car that you actually wanted) for a demo with a few more features that you really don't need or want and a driving history that is somewhat unknown.

In my experience, <u>here is how most demos get sold</u>: a customer comes to the dealership and decides on a specific model, trim level, and color. The salesperson or sales manager then approaches the customer with an alternative: *"We have a demo that has some additional features that we could get you for the same price/payment. Would you like to consider it?"* Now, if you really wanted the car with leather seats and the demo is the only way you can fit it into your budget, this might be your lucky day, however, be aware that this switch is being offered because it benefits the dealership.

4 TEN MISTAKES TO AVOID WHEN VISITING A DEALERSHIP

Mistake #1
Arriving Unprepared
I guess it's obvious you should arrive prepared but many people don't know how to be prepared for a visit to the showroom. Here's the basic stuff you must have done before arriving:
- Have a list of the vehicles that you have researched either online or from recommendations by family and friends and what I mean is Make, Model, Trim, and Package if possible. For example, Make = **Mazda**, Model = **CX-5**, Trim = **GX**, and Package = **Convenience Package**. In this example, a Mazda CX-5 sells for between $22,995 and $35,290 (depending on the Trim and Package). That's a big difference in price and features. Make sure you know what ballpark you are playing in.
- Use the "build and price" tool available on the manufacturer's website (as well as on most dealership websites) to understand the Models, Trims, and Packages as well as what lease or finance payment is reasonable for the Make, Model, and Trim level you have on your list.
- Have a list of questions. Regardless of how much research you do in advance, you should have questions that you need answered in order to clarify some aspects of the vehicle, the financing, the warranties on the vehicle, or the availability of the model on your list. Remember, there are no stupid questions, however, by asking questions that address your particular concerns, you will quickly discover whether the salesperson you meet at the dealership is someone you want to do business with. Incomplete answers or

outright evasion of questions will be the sign that you should be shopping elsewhere. If you have arrived prepared but the salesperson is not ready to answer all your questions and concerns, it's a good predictor that the rest of the process is not going to go smoothly. Find someone you feel is qualified to provide the level of service you deserve.

Mistake #2
Bypassing the Used Car Lot

When I bought my first car, it was a new car and I kicked myself for the next 5 years for making such a stupid decision. But, in those days, the only way to finance a car was to go to the bank and get a car loan, and, the rates were not very "competitive" because there was really no competition for car loans. As a result, I was saddled with a short amortization period and car payments that ate up most of my disposable income. But, I had a shiny new car to drive!

In those days, I probably would have been better off to buy a used car, fix it up, and save myself interest costs and have money for other things. Today, however, the cars and the financing options are much different. On today's motor vehicles (even if they are 5 or 6 years old), the amount of electronics and computer equipment makes doing your own repairs and maintenance almost impossible. Cars now are safer and more reliable but if something goes wrong, they are a lot more expensive to fix. I remember tuning carburetors, checking the spark plug timing, and doing oil changes. Other than oil changes, you need a laptop computer and the manufacturer's software to do the other routine chores. And, by the way, carburetors are now only found in museums.

<u>So, Are You Better to Buy a Pre-Owned Car, or a New Car?</u>

First time car buyers have a choice of buying a brand new car, or buying a used car. Which is better? There are advantages and disadvantages to either choice. Most people would rather have a brand new car with its new-car smell and latest style, but there are reasons that a new car might not be the best choice. Let's take a look at the pros and cons of buying new and buying used.

<u>Advantages of Buying New</u>
• You get a brand new car with new-car feel and smell
• You get the latest styling, technology, and safety equipment
• You get a full manufacturer's warranty

- You get the option to lease
- You may get special manufacturer-sponsored pricing and low rate financing

Disadvantages of Buying New
- The value of a new car depreciates rapidly in the first year or two
- Insurance rates may be higher than for a used car
- Taxes may be higher

Advantages of Buying Used
- You save the high first-year depreciation of value
- If you buy almost-new, you may get the same styling and technology as a new car, at a lower price
- You get price flexibility by choosing between different model years, mileage, and condition
- You may buy "certified" vehicles with inspection and warranty – at a higher cost
- You get lower sales tax

Disadvantages of Buying Used
- You buy "as-is" unless some manufacturer warranty remains
- You may be buying someone else's problem, unless you have your vehicle inspected
- You risk buying a wrecked or salvage vehicle, unless you run a <u>CarProof</u> or <u>CarFax</u> Vehicle History Report
- You typically don't have a lease option
- You may pay higher interest rates if you finance the car
- You may get fewer safety features that are otherwise available on current cars

Summary
To summarize, buying a used car can be a better value for your money but it comes with higher risks. Any used car purchase should include an extensive test drive, an inspection by a qualified mechanic, and a CarFax or CarProof Vehicle History Report. (CarProof is the Canadian standard and CarFax covers the US). Also consider buying an extended warranty (preferably from the vehicle manufacturer). If you're considering an almost-new vehicle, make sure you can't get the same vehicle, new, at about the same price, which can happen if the manufacturer is offering special promotional deals (particularly at the end of the model year).

My Opinion on the Debate

Even though I regretted it on my first car, I believe that conditions now favor buying <u>new</u> over used for most people most of the time. The exception occurs if you are paying <u>cash</u>. You can save real dollars by buying a two-year-old car and having the original owner effectively paying for the depreciation. But if you finance the used car, it's very likely that the depreciation you saved on the purchase will be offset by the higher interest you will pay on a used car loan. New cars are coming with financing rates as low as 0% plus you may qualify for one or more special incentives provided by the manufacturer such as a Loyalty Rebate, or Grad Rebate, or First Time Buyer Rebate, or one of several other incentives. Most of these perks are not available on used cars.

For someone <u>buying a first car</u>, the availability of very low interest rates on terms as long as 84 and 96 months on new cars means you can spread your payments out so your monthly commitment is low but the option of repaying the loan earlier is still available. This way, you get to drive a new car with the newest technologies without handcuffing yourself with unmanageable car payments.

Mistake #3
Failing to Take an Extended Test Drive

When you are in the market for a new vehicle, there is only so much research you can do online. At some point, you need to take your short list of vehicles and see how they fit and feel. No matter how the car looks on paper, if it doesn't connect with you in terms of comfort, ride, handling, or aesthetics, you will likely end up regretting your decision later.

Here are some things you should keep in mind as you head out to test drive your potential new vehicles.

- **Schedule Enough Time**. Take an afternoon or several evenings to do your test-drives and book a time with your salesperson so she or he can have the correct vehicle ready when you arrive. Don't book 4 or 5 test-drives back to back or you may find yourself rushed and/or unable to remember one vehicle from the other.
- **Ask Questions**. A good salesperson should be able to answer your questions about anything you're unfamiliar with. She or he can help you learn how to operate special features such as the Bluetooth system and should be ready to demonstrate how these features work on the test drive.
- **Set Your Route**. Discuss your route with the salesperson before you leave the lot. Try to drive through a range of landscapes during the test so you get a sense of how the car handles in different circumstances such as busy city streets, open highways, hills,

bumps and tight corners. Your salesperson should have such a route already mapped out.

- **Comfort Quotient**. What are headroom and legroom like? Do you bump your head when you get in? Can you adjust your seat and seat belt to your satisfaction? Do the interior proportions feel right? Can you easily read the instrument panel and reach all the controls? Do they feel like they are of high quality? And, don't forget about sightlines and blind spots. Some cars look great from the outside but driver ergonomics and visibility issues can make the day-to-day use of the vehicle enjoyable or dreadful. Only an actual test drive will make it possible to answer these questions fully.
- **Give it a Workout**. Try as many manoeuvres as you can to see how the car handles. Find a quiet street or empty parking lot to test quick stops, acceleration and turning radius. Is the vehicle responsive? Can you control it easily? Also, include a turning circle test on the test drive. If you can turn it 180 degrees on a side street in one movement, the car should be nimble enough for most situations you will encounter.
- **Listen**. Don't let the salesperson's pitch distract you from focusing on the drive: it's okay to ask for a quiet time to just listen to the car. In fact, during the test drive, the salesperson should only be speaking when you have questions to ask. (That's why I prefer to be on the test drive with customers because questions or concerns can be dealt with at the time when they come up). Turn off the radio too, so you can listen for any unusual engine or road noises.
- **Drive it Twice**. Don't hesitate to go away and think about your experience before returning to the dealership for another test drive. It's better to be sure than to live with nagging doubts. At the same time, once you take the car on a complete test drive, you should know pretty quickly whether there is a "connection" with the vehicle. Some customers agonize over which car to choose (even when they have found the perfect car) because they believe there might be another vehicle out there that is even "more perfect". I believe you will usually find that, when you find it, you'll know it.

Because there is no shortage of quality vehicles on the market today, your goal of test-driving a few short-listed vehicles is to determine (in a reasonably rational process) whether one car really "speaks to you". If you make a "connection" with a car that passes the above tests, it's a good sign that you have found that special vehicle that you will enjoy owning for years to come.

Mistake #4
Not Booking an Appointment

I recently booked an appointment with my doctor. I gave him an indication of the reason for the visit when I booked the appointment so he was prepared for our meeting. The time we spent together was not long but the assistance and advice I received was extremely helpful and actionable. During our meeting, I had the doctor's <u>undivided attention</u>. I only wish that a larger portion of the people coming to the dealership would take this approach. It works in most other situations where you are making a major purchase or decision and are seeking expertise and assistance.

Many of the people who buy cars from me book an appointment (if not to buy the car) to get advice on what vehicle or lease/financing option would best suit their needs. Because our dealership is in a high traffic auto-mall, many people coming to our store, just arrive at random. I am always puzzled by people who wander from dealership to dealership when they are in the market for a car. It does not seem to be the most productive use of one's time (unless, of course, you have read this guide in which case you will be well armed to handle any situation that you encounter).

If you want to talk to the <u>most experienced and knowledgeable people at the dealership</u>, your chances of meeting one by just wandering in are pretty limited. Chances are higher that you will be "picked up" by one of the junior sales people on the floor whose product knowledge is sketchy and whose assessment skills are in the development stage (despite how enthusiastic they might be). Meanwhile, the senior sales people are busy meeting with prospects who have booked appointments.

Most people in the market for a car do some research online and talk to friends or family about what brands or models should be considered. ***You probably have two or three cars on your short list***. This is the point where <u>I always recommend that you contact a dealership or a specific car salesperson recommended by someone you trust</u>. Or, contact your local dealership to find an experienced professional to assist you. You can call the sales manager and ask that you be put in touch with the dealership's best sales consultant. Or simply <u>go to the dealership website</u> and complete one of the forms for information on the model of interest.

When you inquire online, you will normally be dealing with one of the senior sales people at the dealership (as most car dealerships have online requests handled by the <u>Internet Manager</u>). Now, you can get some basic questions answered before you book an appointment. When you arrive at the dealership, you have someone specific to meet and the sales consultant can have the specific models of interest lined up for you to consider. The other advantage of handling your car buying process in this way is that <u>you are dealing with a member of the dealership management</u> who is equipped to find all the manufacturer incentives for which you qualify as well as having **the authority to work out a special deal for you** that might not otherwise be available to someone just walking in off the street.

If you want to be treated like a V.I.P., it's best to book an appointment just like you would if you were planning to buy a house, setting up a program with a fitness trainer, or taking a golf lesson. Or, you can wander into a dealership at random and hope you get lucky.

Mistake #5
Not Researching the Value of Your Trade-in Vehicle

Among the early lessons my father taught me about economics was that <u>things are worth what someone is willing to pay for them</u>. When it's time to trade or sell a pre-owned vehicle, car owners obviously want the maximum value for it. At the very least, they want fair market value. Sometimes it's difficult to separate the emotional value (i.e., only you know what a wonderful car it's been for the past 10 years and 250,000 Km) from the economic value.

But "fair market value" (or economic value) often differs from the perceived value that a customer has in mind. In fact, customers are frequently disappointed to learn their vehicles are worth less than they anticipated — sometimes several thousand dollars less.

Many factors go into determining what a dealership (or a private buyer) will pay for a vehicle, including the original MSRP (Manufacturer's Suggested Retail Price), mechanical condition, physical appearance, mileage, market conditions, accessories, brand, model type, maintenance history, accident history, etc.

To avoid a shock when you get to the dealership and have your trade-in appraised, I suggest customers take 5 minutes to check out the trade-in value of their vehicle on **CanadianBlackBook.com**. You can plug in the year, make, model, mileage, and equipment on your vehicle and quickly get a range of what is being paid (in your geographic area) for comparable vehicles (by dealers). I get a lot of customers who check prices on **Autotrader** (which provides a listing of what private sellers and dealers are

asking for used vehicles). Remember, these are <u>retail prices</u> for certified and re-conditioned (if bought at a dealership) vehicles, whereas your trade-in is an **As Is**, uncertified vehicle being sold <u>wholesale</u>.

If you arrive at the dealership with a reasonable idea of the wholesale and retail values for your vintage vehicle, you are better able to negotiate a fair price. If your vehicle is accident-free and in good condition, you are in a position to hold out for a price at the higher end of the value range. If the used car manager feels your trade-in can be put on the lot without major reconditioning costs, he will often be persuaded to pay a little above "fair market value" for your trade-in if it is the key to closing the deal on the new vehicle.

Mistake #6
Landing on the Wrong Car (for your needs)

Whenever you sit down with a sales consultant at a car dealership, you can expect to be asked a lot of questions. By the way, if it feels like an interrogation, you're not sitting with a true professional. ***A good salesperson will want to have a <u>conversation</u> where he/she learns about your situation, what kind of cars you have owned until now, and get an idea of the kind of vehicle that might fit your needs and desires at this point in your life.*** The better the salesperson understands your situation, the better he/she can help you select the car that is perfect for you. It might even be a model or trim package that your had not considered but is a great fit.

Now, if your reaction is to be a bit suspicious about car salespeople anyway, you might find answering a lot of questions to be uncomfortable and somewhat intrusive. Rather than being offended, you should consider this as a mark of a trained sales professional who is interested in you as well as in matching you up with a vehicle that fits your lifestyle and budget. Despite the fact that you may have checked out the various trim levels and packages online, a good salesperson will be able to make suggestions (either product or financing related) that may not have been evident in your online research.

When I meet with customers for the first time (whether in person at the dealership or online), I am most interested in understanding: **What transportation problem are you trying to solve?** To understand this, I need to know what you are driving now (maybe you're taking the bus), what vehicles are already in the household, what's been happening with your shopping experience so far, and what information you already have (as well as what information you still need to feel comfortable about making a decision).

These are questions you should be asking yourself as well. Why is your car falling a bit short of what you need? It's also helpful to know if anything in your life has changed recently (or is about to change) where you need something different or better. And, since you have arrived at our showroom, what is it about our brand, model, or dealership that you believe might make it the best choice? With this information, which only takes a few minutes to acquire, I am in a pretty good position to pick out a couple of product alternatives that will fit the bill. The alternative is to guess and spend time considering and test driving several models only to discover we are on the wrong car. Since that's not much fun for you nor the salesperson, it's much better to take a little time up front and clarify the transportation problem you came to the dealership to solve.

Mistake #7
Letting the Emotion of the Situation Overtake Your Judgment
It is easy to take this caution lightly and think to yourself, "Don't worry, I am quite capable of handling my emotions, thank you!". However, the modern car dealership and the people who work there have developed a process that is pretty effective in moving most people from calm and cool to excited and ready to agree to things they might otherwise vigorously scrutinize. Every step of the process has been planned and choreographed in advance to move you from a mildly interested shopper to an enthusiastic buyer. It's OK to enjoy the "ride" as long as you do not lose sight of the fact that the whole process is rigged to get you to buy a car today. If you are open to that possibility (because you have prepared for your visit), then have some fun but keep one hand on your wallet. At the end of the process, you want to make an informed and rational decision but you can do that and still have fun in the process.

Mistake #8
Blowing Your Budget (or Not Having a Budget)
As is the case with any major purchase, it is not uncommon to end up spending more than you expected by the time the process is completed. In fact, I would be surprised if you went car shopping with a rough idea of what you expected to pay and actually came in under your "budget". It almost never happens that way. The truth is, everything costs more than what we expect and what we want to pay for it. Nevertheless, it is your responsibility to sketch out, in advance, the monthly outflows that a new car will involve and decide where your "comfort zone" ends. Here's the list of cash costs to tally:

- Finance/Lease payments (including all taxes and fees)
- Insurance Coverage. Talk to your insurance company or broker in advance and ask about the cars on your short list and what coverage will be needed as well as the cost. (Some cars are cheaper to insure than others)
- Gas & Maintenance. If this is your first car, you may be trading bus fare for gas station charges. Now, if you are moving from an old car to a new car, you should find that the improved mileage will save you on gas. Maintenance expenses on a new car should be near zero for the first few years (as the manufacturer's standard warranties will cover anything serious) but maintenance on used cars starts to accelerate once they get past 4 years old.
- Savings. Also consider that there should be gas savings, possibility insurance savings, and maintenance savings that will result from moving from an old clunker to a new (or newer) car. Those should also be factored into your monthly budget.

Sometimes, car buyers get stuck on a monthly number that they have set and are reluctant to exceed it by even a dollar. Usually, you will find that the car you really want will put you over your budget. That's why you should have a budget but also <u>consider what you could live with</u> if you found the absolutely perfect vehicle. If you allow for this possibility in your planning, you have a better chance of getting exactly the car you want without blowing the budget (maybe just stretching it a bit).

Mistake #9
Saying You are "Not Buying Today"

Based on my experience in the car business and the evolution I have been seeing recently in <u>manufacturers and dealers becoming more focused on delighting and retaining customers</u>, I offer the following suggestions that I guarantee will get you a great deal without wasting time:

- **<u>Arrive at the dealership as a buyer</u>**. Too often, car buyers get off on the wrong foot by coming to a dealership and indicating very early that they have no plans to buy today. The experienced car sales professional is not put off by your "not buying today" declaration but they will consider it a challenge to overcome. What you want to avoid is a confrontational encounter so your best strategy when buying a car is to identify yourself as a buyer, not a shopper. Don't be defensive; simply present yourself as an easy buyer to deal with. The customer who approaches a car dealer in a defensive and pushy manner, tends to cause the dealership personnel to respond the same way. If you want to play games,

there is no shortage of salespeople capable of operating in that realm. Make it clear you are ready to buy and watch how well you get treated.
- **Price should not be your greatest concern**. Let the salesperson know that price is not your biggest concern but that the car is your main focus. This will be well received by the salesperson and encourage them to provide the full level of service you deserve. Let them know that you know that agreeing on price is easy once the car is right. This is going to make the sales process quicker by reducing confrontation and later, will make getting your best possible terms even easier.
- **Determine the right car for you**. Contrary to strategies of the past, the best way to determine the right vehicle is not online or on the phone but at the dealership. A trick to make sure you are on the right vehicle is to look at the vehicles just above and just below what you think you want. Any interest you have in either of the other two product choices means you are not yet on the perfect product for you. Before you go further, make sure you have identified the car that is exactly what you need and want.
- **Test-drive the vehicle**. Driving the vehicle will actually save you time negotiating and makes the dealership feel like they have done their job and provides them with more confidence in giving you their best price. Besides, until you drive the vehicle, you cannot know if it feels like the vehicle you want to be spending a lot of time with for the next 5 or 10 years.
- **Request a fully documented proposal**. Ask the dealership to present their offer to you including price, trade figures, purchase and lease payments, down payments and interest rates as well as rebates and incentives that you are qualified to receive, all at one time.
- **Determining a fair price?** Franchised car dealers in Canada and the US operate on about the same net margins as a grocery store (i.e., 2% net margin - after all expenses). Most transactions generate more money to government taxes than profits to the dealer. For instance, the taxes in Ontario are 13% (HST), so if the dealer has a gross mark up (before expenses) of 6% on a $20,000 car, they will have a gross profit of $1,200 while the government will collect over $2,600. Keep in mind the province of Ontario isn't even in the car business. Based on this reality, use your own logic to make sense of what is a fair price to offer the dealer. Your dealer will love this logic and remove time and pain from the process.

It is outdated thinking to believe that you have to shop 5 or 6 locations to get a good deal. The next time you are ready to get something new just follow my steps; let your dealer know you are there to buy, be sure you are on the right car, ask that they present their proposal in writing, and lastly, enter the discussion of value and pricing issues with a positive and respectful attitude and I guarantee you a great deal!

Mistake #10
"Just Give Me Your Best Price"

On a fairly regular basis, some of our less sophisticated shoppers come to the dealership asking for our **"best price"**. <u>By asking this question in a dealership, it is almost certain that you will not get the dealership's "best price" (whatever that means to you)</u>. Perhaps these people believe there is a secret no-go-below price on each vehicle that has been pre-determined by the owner and by just boldly asking for it, they will get it. On the contrary, I can guarantee you that no such list exists.

The truth is that we have the **Manufacturer's Suggested Retail Price** (MSRP) and we have the **dealer cost** (which is what the dealership paid the manufacturer for the car). **Somewhere between these two numbers is a number that the dealership will agree to accept**, however, <u>this number will vary depending on a number of factors (some of which change by day and by week)</u>. For example, let's say the dealership has a new car in a color that has been unpopular and the sales manager just got a lecture from the owner earlier that day that inventory turnover is below standard (based on the aged inventory report just run). If someone comes into the store interested in that particular vehicle today (in the hard-to-sell color), he might agree to move that vehicle at any firm offer above dealer cost to get the inventory moving in the right direction. On the same car in a more popular color, he might not be so flexible.

Of course, <u>the dealership's</u> "best price" is the MSRP (where they make a fair but not excessive profit) and <u>the dealership's</u> "worst price" is the dealer cost where they make nothing on the car. Sometimes, dealerships will sell a car at their "worst price" for a variety of reasons including the one mentioned above. For example, **it's the end of the month and the sales manager needs a few more deals to hit a target for the month** (maybe that target represents a sales bonus). Or, it is the last day of a major sales event on which the owner has spent a considerable amount on advertising and promotion. It's easier for the sales manager to explain that a few of the deals were "skinny" than to explain why the target was missed (by a few units). That's how the business works in the real world.

The concept of "Supply and Demand" also plays into determining the "best price". Cars that are in short supply are seldom discounted while those that the dealer knows are backed up on lots across the district are more likely to be discounted (beyond the incentives provided by the manufacturer). <u>It is difficult for the average car shopper to know (by brand and by dealership) what dynamics are at work on a particular day or week</u>. By the same token, it is difficult for the salesperson (or even the sales manager) to know what crazy deal he/she might ultimately agree to do until <u>faced with a serious buyer on a particular car</u> that he/she has been trying to sell for months.

If you are a car buyer and you find yourself in such a situation where you are on a car that the sales manager feels "must" be sold and you have negotiated a great deal, you should take advantage of the leverage you have and do the deal. I have seen customers walk away from outstanding opportunities where they had the sales manager over-a-barrel because they wanted to "think about it" only to return a day or two later to find the deal had been taken off the table (when the sales manager had returned to his/her senses). By the way, in most jurisdictions, it's only a "deal" when both parties have signed a purchase agreement.

And one last point, **the salesperson's job is <u>not</u> to negotiate a discounted price**. <u>His/her job is to understand your vehicle needs and get you on a vehicle well suited to those needs</u> (as well as to select a car that is affordable for you). The latter is a bit imprecise so if there is a disconnect between the regular price of the car and the price that the customer is willing to pay, the sales manager has the final authority. That's why <u>the salesperson will ask you for a formal signed offer</u> if you believe the price presented is unacceptable. If you caught the sales manager on the right day and right vehicle, you might find your offer accepted.

5 A FEW OTHER IMPORTANT MATTERS TO CONSIDER

The Importance of Value and Price

Not all makes and models in the same vehicle category are created equal. Similarly equipped Honda Civic, Toyota Corolla, Mazda3, Volkswagen Jetta, Ford Focus and Hyundai Elantra vehicles will be priced about the same and the incentives, over time, will be similar, however, the safety systems are not equal, the crash test results will be different, the driving dynamics will be different, the future re-sale value will be different, the cost to insure will be different, the styling will be different, driver ergonomics will be different, and the fuel economy will be different. So, if the price of each vehicle is the same, what are you going to do to make a decision? In other words, what characteristics do you value most?

Think about what is most important to you before venturing off to the dealership so you can evaluate the vehicles you test drive based on the important criteria that you have already set.

Steps to the Sale/Purchase

The sales process that I talked about earlier has been around for a long time and includes the following steps in roughly this order. It is the goal of the salesperson to move you through this process so, by the end of the process, you are "conditioned" to say "Yes" to buying a car today. Here are the steps you can expect:

1. <u>Meet & Greet</u>. The object here is to build rapport and move you from cautious to accepting because the dealership knows that people buy from people they know, like, and trust so this is the beginning of building that relationship. If it's genuine, that's a

bonus.
2. <u>Qualify & Counsel</u>. The more the salesperson knows about your (transportation) situation and other things going on in your life, the better he/she is able to select a vehicle that fits your needs and your budget. You may have a particular vehicle in mind but, based on this conversation, there way be other vehicles that would work for you. (This is particularly true when dealing with Used Cars where every dealership lot has a unique assortment of vehicles).
3. <u>Vehicle Selection</u>. The salesperson will want to land you on a specific vehicle to focus the discussion since trying to consider three or four vehicles at once is a recipe for indecision. It is probably in both your interest (as well as the salesperson's) to fix on one vehicle at this point to simplify things and focus the conversation. You can always go back to consider other vehicles if the selected vehicle does not turn out to be the best fit.
4. <u>Vehicle Presentation</u>. Here is the salesperson's opportunity to "pitch" the selected vehicle and talk about the features, benefits, and advantages important to you (discerned from the Qualify stage). This is where the good salesperson will build excitement and involve you in the presentation so you start moving toward "mental ownership".
5. <u>Vehicle Demonstration</u>. The best way to find out about the vehicle is to test drive it. This is where your emotions are stimulated and you start to "connect" with the vehicle (assuming it is the right vehicle for you).
6. <u>Transition</u>. As you return to the dealership, the salesperson will try to gauge your interest level and readiness to proceed by asking questions that move you toward a commitment. This is also the point where your trade-in vehicle (if you have one) will be checked and discussed (if it was not done earlier in the process). This is where you will get a trial close such as "So, if we can get the numbers to work out, are you prepared to move ahead today?"
7. <u>Facility Tour</u>. For many customers, the vehicle is only part of the transaction, so the salesperson's job is to sell the whole package of benefits (of doing business with this dealership and this salesperson). The facility tour, including introductions to some of the people you will be dealing with, is part of offering more than just a car and a price. Once you start to see this as a long-term relationship with the dealership and its staff, you are much closer to agreeing to buy the car (that the test drive demonstrated was the perfect solution to your transportation problem).
8. <u>Trial Close – Commitment</u>. This is the point where the salesperson must determine if you are willing to commit to buying

the car if any concerns or "objections' you have raised can be dealt with. For the salesperson, there is no point in providing you with a detailed proposal(s) if it is clear you are not prepared to make a decision. The reason is quite simple; the dealership can only assume that your intention is to take their proposal and "shop it" around town to see if a better deal is possible. This why it does not help your negotiating position to say you want to think about it or that you indeed plan to continue shopping. Most dealerships will not make a proposal unless they feel there is a reasonable possibility you will accept it.
9. <u>Proposal</u>. The dealership will put together two or three proposals based on what they can afford and based on what they believe you are willing to pay. These will normally take the form of monthly payments under a couple of different scenarios such as different terms, down payments, or lease versus buy options. They should line up with what the salesperson has been able to discover about your budget and other requirements.
10. <u>Close the Sale</u>. Once you have a proposal in front of you and the vehicle meets or exceeds your requirements, the next step is to make a counter-proposal. Never accept the dealership's initial proposal. If you are reasonable, it will likely be accepted.

Should You Lease or Buy?

Leasing of cars fell off substantially following the <u>financial crisis of 2008/2009</u>, however, it has recovered to over 25% of sales in Canada (and over 50% for some brands and dealerships). For a segment of the car buying public, <u>leasing has always made a lot of sense</u> and now, more of the general public is coming back to this form of financing.

Despite some attitudes that continue to prevail, **<u>leasing is simply a finance option that closely matches the customer's buying cycle</u>**, allowing you to continually be driving a relatively new vehicle. The other big benefit that people have started to realize in recent years is that **<u>leasing eliminates the risk of negative equity!</u>** When you come to the end of your 36-month or 48-month lease, you either jump into a new lease or walk away (with no further obligation) or buy out the vehicle at a pre-determined price. <u>If you were 3 or 4 years into an 84 month financing</u>, you would likely be in a **negative equity situation**, i.e., the car would be <u>worth less than what you still owe</u> the bank on your car loan.

Low financing rates offered by manufacturers in recent years for extended terms (up to 84 months) have <u>seduced consumers into buying cars that would otherwise be out of their reach</u>. If your intention is to keep the car for ten years, this strategy can have some logic but how many people's circumstances remain the same for 8 to 10 years? Once you are into that long term commitment, you had better hope that you do not get into a major accident (automatically lowers the car's trade-in value), or experience a major change in your family situation (all of a sudden you're in the wrong car for your situation), or experience a major component breakdown just beyond the warranty period (which makes the case for extended warranty coverage to match your extended financing).

According to Edmunds.com, maintenance costs in years 4, 5, and 6, **average $100 to $150 per month** for a mid-sized sedan. Most manufacturers' standard comprehensive warranty matches the most common lease terms and mileage. If you keep leasing, you'll always have a monthly payment but you avoid major repair bills indefinitely.

The critical question if you are considering a lease is the difference in your position at trade-in time! Let's assume you are a high mileage driver. (That is usually the argument for not leasing). On a Lease, Mazda's excess kilometer penalty is 8 cents per km on all vehicles except the CX-9. On a standard 3 Year/ 72,000 kilometer lease, **adding 40,000 extra Km x $0.08 = $3,200**. If you have two 3-year-old cars (one at 72,000 km and another at 112,000 Km), how much lower will the appraisal on the higher mileage car be? Think about it. That's why it looks like **leasing makes sense for the low mileage and the high mileage driver!**

Before you get hypnotized by that low 84-month financing, consider if leasing might make sense for you. Leasing is back and you owe it to yourself to consider this financing option when you are shopping for your next car.

Fuel Saving Technologies – A Short Primer on How to Not Be Confused

Car manufacturers are all required by international environmental agreements and national laws passed in Europe and North America to limit emissions and improve overall fuel economy in order to sell cars in these jurisdictions. Each has come up with different ways to achieve those requirements and each technology has benefits and drawbacks that consumers should be aware of as they try to select a vehicle and a technology solution.

Here are the major fuel saving technologies you will encounter and some thoughts on their benefits and drawbacks:

- *Hybrid Vehicles*. The solution that many car companies found easiest to develop was the hydrid vehicle which involves downsizing the gasoline engine and adding an electric motor and battery packs. The electric motor "assists" the gasoline engine so performance is not too severely compromised, however, the added weight of the batteries and the somewhat sluggish acceleration results in a vehicle that is heavy and has mediocre handling characteristics. Hybrids are also still more expensive than conventional vehicles meaning the fuel savings may not be offset by the difference in gas mileage.

- *Continuously Variable Transmissions* (CVT). The CVT is becoming an increasingly common form of automatic transmission. It is inexpensive to build for the car manufacturer and helps improve gas mileage because the heavy-duty drive chain allows the engine to always be operating in the "sweet spot" for minimum fuel consumption. The big drawback is noisy and sluggish performance along with the absence of a sense of being connected to the road or the wheels.

- *Dual Clutch Transmissions.* With these new transmissions, you have two separate automated manual gearboxes, each with its own clutch, but one containing the odd gears and the other the even ones. Therefore, as you're accelerating, each gearbox readies the next gear up. Dual-clutch automatics tend to offer snappy, coordinated shifts when you're driving quickly as well as a little more driving enjoyment than a typical automatic. Because of their light-weight and low-friction operation, dual clutch systems also help to save gas but are not a drag on performance.

- *Turbo-Charged*. Another way to get more power from a smaller engine is to use turbocharging as Ford has been doing on their

Ford EcoBoost vehicles. This process is a combination of turbocharging and direct fuel injection that improves fuel economy without sacrificing engine power. Smaller engines use less gas so the EcoBoost solution delivers improved gas mileage without giving up performance.

- ***SKYACTIV.*** Mazda's SKYACTIV solution uses direct fuel injection along with a high compression engine (instead of turbocharging) to generate increased horsepower and torque from smaller engines. It also combines the high compression engine with a dual clutch transmission and lightweight unibody structure to reduce weight which all combines to generate close-to-hybrid gas mileage but improved handling and overall performance.
- ***Diesel.*** Vehicles that run on diesel fuel are a clear choice for great fuel economy with the added benefit that they provide lots of torque. Diesel fuel prices are similar to gasoline in North America, meaning you will save money at the pump, however, diesel vehicles will normally cost you a couple of thousand dollars more to own. In Canada, only Chevrolet, Dodge, Mercedes, Audi, BMW and Volkswagen currently offer diesel passenger vehicles.
- ***Hydrogen Fuel Cell.*** A potential for the future, this zero-emissions technology promises to cut driving costs drastically, however, the lack of hydrogen filling station infrastructure means this solution is still a long shot.
- ***Electric.*** Electric Vehicles (E.V.) are not new. By 1900, 28% of vehicles produced in the U.S. were powered by electricity. Now, they are making a comeback (although with government subsidy help). Their high cost and limited range have, so far, limited their popularity, however, the rapid advancements in battery technologies is changing the game.

Invoice Services and How to Use Them Wisely

The best way to save money and know exactly what kind of a deal you are getting is to use an Invoice Service which makes it possible to cut through all the confusion and complexities that have traditionally been part of working a great car deal. If you know what the dealer paid for the car you are considering, it should make it easier to come to terms that you consider fair.

In Canada, you can subscribe to the following services to obtain dealer cost information (along with any special factory rebates, allowances, or incentives) for the specific vehicle you are considering:

- **CarCostCanada** (www.CarCostCanada.com) is a subsidiary of Armada Insurance and provides up to five reports for $39.95. The information is accurate although it requires some familiarity with the vehicle(s) under consideration to determine the dealer's cost. Most dealers will ask you to pay 3% to 4% above the dealer cost but you will still qualify for any/all incentives that the manufacturer has made available to regular customers.

- **Unhaggle** (www.unhaggle.com) has two services available. You can secure a report on a vehicle (just like CarCostCanada), however, the service is free. Dealers who have signed up with Unhaggle pay for your contact information when you pull a report and will be sure to be contacting you right away. One of the reasons to go with Unhaggle is because they have pre-screened dealerships by brand and region so you will be directed to a dealership that has met Unhaggle's standards for transparency and customer service quality. (Of course, you can take the information and work with any dealer). Unhaggle also has a bidding service where you pay a fee (about 1% of the vehicle price) and your preferred vehicle choice will be sent to several dealers who will submit closed bids on the exact vehicle (or the closest available substitute) and you simply select the lowest bidder and go to the dealer to sign the paperwork and pick up the car.

- **Automobile Protection Association** (www.apa.com) The APA has a New Vehicle Buying Service that has been in operation for many years where they take your vehicle order and shop it around various dealers to find the best deal. Once you pay their fee, you may not be much further ahead than getting an Unhaggle report or CCC report and walking into a dealership with an offer of cost plus 3%. The benefit is that the APA will save you time and effort.

- **Canadian Automobile Association** (www.caa.ca) If you are a member of your local CAA, you can use your membership card to get discounts from affiliate dealers, however, many (perhaps, most) dealers are not affiliate members in which case you are just another customer.

In the United States, there are similar but different invoice services that you can contact to obtain dealer cost information for the specific vehicle you are considering:
- **TrueCar** (www.TrueCar.com) uses "certified" dealers and when it started out, would provide the following information for the vehicle you specified in your geographic area: Dealer Cost, Average Paid, Factory Invoice, and Sticker Price. However, because of pressure from car manufacturers and dealers, TrueCar has dropped the Dealer Cost portion and now only offers the factory invoice along with the average paid meaning you are not getting the information needed to determine if you are getting the best available deal. (It may be a fair deal but not likely the best). You should note that other car buying services are powered by TrueCar so the same comments apply to them. Among the firms partnered with True Car are USAA, Consumer Reports, AAA, and AARP.
- **Edmunds** (Edmunds.com) You can use Edmunds.com to get the MSRP (Manufacturer's Suggested Retail Price) as well as the average price paid for a specific vehicle in your Zip Code which is an easy and low cost way to determine what would be a fair deal but you still won't know if it's the best available deal.
- **Cars Direct** (www.CarsDirect.com) will act as a broker to negotiate on your behalf for the specific vehicle you want in your Zip Code or they will direct you to the Internet Manager at a dealer in your area along with price guidance that you can use for a hassle-free purchase.
- **Kelley Blue Book** (www.kbb.com) provides what they call "Fair Purchase Price" on any vehicle you select in your Zip Code. It is not clear how they determine this price, however, it is better than the MSRP but higher than the Dealer Invoice Price.

If you are buying a car in Canada, it is a complete waste of time to use a U.S. based service to determine a fair price because the pricing structure, the legislation governing vehicle sales, and the way the vehicle trims and packages are set up are often completely different from one country to the next. And, if you are trying to figure out what the dealer's true cost is, the difference in terminology (between Canada and the U.S.) will make the exercise even more confusing. In the U.S., the "Invoice Price" does not refer to the actual cost paid by the dealer. That's why it is possible (in the U.S.) to buy a car at "below invoice" (because various manufacturer "hold backs" are not on the invoice but can be determined). In Canada, the "dealer net price" is the actual price that the dealer paid for the vehicle. There are, generally, no holdbacks except for bonuses to the dealer if specific volume and customer satisfaction targets are met (monthly, quarterly, and annually).

6 WHAT FEES MUST YOU PAY ON A NEW CAR?

The MSRP (Manufacturer's Suggested Retail Price) is normally readily available on the manufacturer's website for every model, trim level, and package. For example, in Canada, a 2015 Mazda3 GS with automatic transmission and a moonroof (model, trim level, and package) is currently $22,845. On Mazda's website (www.Mazda.ca), you will see a charge for Freight & PDE that totals $1,695 and which must be added to the MSRP.

- The Freight component represents the amount charged by the manufacturer to transport the vehicle from the factory to the dealer's lot. Freight charges vary from model to model (and are currently $1,095 on a Mazda3).
- The PDE (Pre-Delivery Expense) represents the amount that the manufacturer has allowed the dealer to charge for setting up the vehicle for delivery (including all pre-delivery inspections, mechanical set ups, gas fill up, and detailing).

The other fees and taxes that must be paid in Ontario for a new car are:

1. **Air Tax**. The federal government charges an air conditioner excise tax of **$100** (if your vehicle has air conditioning).
2. **OTS Tax**. The Ontario Tire Stewardship fee is charged on all tires to cover the eventual disposal cost for the tires on your car. The government used to charge this only when you disposed of old tires but recently decided it was better to get the money upfront. For passenger vehicles and light trucks, **the fee is $5.43 per tire**. With four tires and a spare on your new car, the fee works out to be **$27.15 as of May 1, 2014**.
3. **Gas Tax**. Ontario used to collect a gas consumption tax which was eliminated when the RST (Retail Sales Tax) was replaced by

the HST (Harmonized Sales Tax).
4. **OMVIC Fee**. The Ontario Motor Vehicle Industry Council is the governing body for car dealership and car salespeople in Ontario. OMVIC collects a **$5 transaction fee** to support its dispute resolution activities.
5. **PPSA Fee**. If you finance or lease a vehicle, the bank or leasing company will charge a fee to set up the loan and register the lien on the vehicle under the requirements of the Personal Property Security Act (PPSA). This fee is usually between **$75 and $150** depending on the amount and the term of the loan. If you pay cash, this charge does not apply.
6. **Licensing**. Most dealerships charge a fee to take care of the licensing of the new vehicle including transferring plates if necessary. The charge is normally about **$25** plus the cost of your sticker plus any outstanding fines.
7. **HST**. Most goods and services in Ontario are subject to the **13% HST** (Harmonized Sales Tax) which replaced the old PST/GST. If you are trading in a vehicle, you only pay HST on the difference between the new car price and the value of your trade-in. (***Most provinces and states have a sales tax that applies to the sale of motor vehicles and operates in the same manner as the Ontario example just illustrated***).

The above fees and taxes are all mandatory and are not subject to negotiation. Dealers, however, often provide other additional products and/or services that are designed to increase the profit on the vehicle being sold. On these items, you can choose to purchase these extras as offered or negotiate to get the price reduced or eliminate them altogether.

- Security Package. Most dealers etch their vehicles with a police traceable code that is part of an insurance policy in case the vehicle gets stolen. You may purchase this protection, however, depending on your current automobile insurance policy, you may already have equivalent coverage from your insurance company. Look for this on your purchase agreement; it may have already been included in the payment quoted. It may be called an "Administration Charge" or it might be one of a number of charges. Always make sure that all charges are disclosed and explained before signing the Purchase Agreement.
- Nitrogen Filled Tires. There are benefits to having your tires filled with 100% nitrogen as it helps maintain constant tire pressures and helps improve tire life. If you buy it, see that you get some kind of road hazard tire warranty with it. And note what is charged for this

extra. Some dealers include it with the security package.
- <u>Wheel Locks</u>. Many cars now come with expensive alloy wheels so most dealers install wheel locks on the vehicle when it arrives on the lot. This is pretty inexpensive insurance against getting these stolen off your vehicle. Dealers usually charge about $75 to install these locks.

There are lots of other products and services that dealers will offer you once you have agreed to purchase a new car. These include rust protection, extended warranty protection, life and disability insurance, loss of employment insurance, tinted windows, and various dealer installed accessories. Always scrutinize these added products or services to determine if the price charged represents good value.

7 WHY YOU WANT A FRIEND IN THE CAR BUSINESS

People tell me that it's great to have **a friend in the car business** because you <u>want</u> to have a friend and advisor when you're in the process of buying a car. It's not easy figuring out what transportation solutions make the most sense. After all, you're trying to juggle what you <u>need</u>, what you <u>want</u>, and what you can <u>afford</u>. So, my job is to help you sort through those issues. I hope this guide has been helpful in getting you through some of the complexities.

Since I got into the car business about 8 years ago, I have helped hundreds of people solve their transportation problems by bringing <u>integrity</u>, <u>transparency</u>, and <u>compassion</u> to the process of finding and financing a quality new or used car.

As you may have discovered as you read this guide, I sell Mazda vehicles, so that is my product bias, but I am happy to answer <u>any car purchase question</u> that you might have. If there is a question that this guide has not addressed, I would encourage you to let me know so I can get you the answer and include the information in future updates. I am always trying to find new and better ways to serve customers.

Hey. Thanks again for reading. I'll see you at the dealership.

Gordon Wright
Your Friend in the Car Business

8 RESOURCES

Most of the references in this Consumer Awareness Guide are based on *buying a car in Ontario, Canada* where the legislation, regulations, and consumer protections are among the most rigorous in North American. If you live in another Canadian Province or in the United States, the principles outlined in this guide still apply, however, your recourse to government agencies to assist you will be different. Here is a list of resources by province and by state:

CANADA

Prov.	Protection for Car Buyers	Vehicle Licensing Authority
BC	Motor Vehicle Sales Authority of B.C. www.mvsabc.com	Insurance Corporation of B.C. www.icbc.com
AB	Alberta Motor Vehicle Industry Council. www.amvic.org	Service Alberta. www.servicealberta.ca
SK	Saskatchewan Motor Dealers Act. www.justice.gov.sk.ca	S.G.I. www.sgi.sk.ca
MB	Manitoba Consumer Protection Office. www.gov.mb.ca/cca/cpo	Manitoba Public Insurance. http://mpi.mb.ca
ON	Ontario Motor Vehicle Industry Council. www.omvic.on.ca	Ministry of Transportation of Ontario. www.mto.gov.on.ca
QC	Consumer Protection Office. www.opc.gouv.gc.ca	S.A.A.Q. www.saaq.gouv.qc.ca/en
NB	Government of Canada Consumer Information.	Service New Brunswick. www.snb.ca/e

	www.consumerinformation.ca	
NS	Government of Canada Consumer Information. www.consumerinformation.ca	Service Nova Scotia. www.novascotia.ca/sns/mv
PE	Government of Canada Consumer Information. www.consumerinformation.ca	Prince Edward Island Transportation & Infrastructure. www.gov.pe.ca/highwaysafety
NL	Government of Canada Consumer Information. www.consumerinformation.ca	Service Newfoundland. www.servicenl.gov.nl.ca
NU	Government of Canada Consumer Information. www.consumerinformation.ca	Government of Nunavut. www.gov.nu.ca/
NW	Government of Canada Consumer Information. www.consumerinformation.ca	North West Territories Depart of Transportation. dmv.dot.gov.nt.ca/vehicle-registration
YK	Government of Canada Consumer Information. www.consumerinformation.ca	Yukon Highways & Public Works. www.hpw.gov.yk.ca/mv/

UNITED STATES

State	Protection for Car Buyers	Vehicle Licensing Authority
All	The "one stop shop" for all questions about your car buying rights by state can be found on this non-government website: www.dmv.org	All state regulations and forms can be found at this single non-government website along with helpful tips. Enter your state and everything you need is easily accessible: www.dmv.org

ABOUT THE AUTHOR

Following a successful 25+ year career in corporate marketing and sales combined with an economic downturn that impacted many in that line of work, Gordon Wright decided to follow a passion and a fascination that went back to his youth in small town Nova Scotia. He always loved cars and he also loved talking about cars. A car dealership looked like the perfect place to bring those elements together. As a marketing professional, he was intrigued by the relationship most of us have with cars. Working as a salesperson on the dealership floor, he started to learn first-hand how the glamour and the reality were often in opposition.

It seemed clear that **people love cars** and **people love to shop** but **they do not love to shop for cars**. He soon discovered that the way dealerships and car sales people are generally trained to conduct business was a lot different than what he had been used to in the corporate world. He soon developed a different approach with customers that was based on the philosophy that an educated buyer is an easier customer to work with. This is how he built a solid base of customers who appreciated his approach.

At the same time, the internet and social media were providing more tools for car buyers to begin to level the playing field. Unfortunately, the industry is still populated by a significant percentage of "old school" thinking in an increasingly competitive industry. The result is that despite some improvements in some quarters, it is still likely that you will be subject to a wide range of deceptive practices and "smoke and mirrors" techniques when you visit a dealership even though you arrive with lots of product information and research.

Gordon Wright pioneered a *New Way to Buy a Car* in the way he conducted business in the showroom and online. He realized that these methods worked better than the "old school" tactics employed by many of his colleagues and was rewarded with many repeat customers and referrals. Educated customers, he found, were happy customers and were eager to spread the word.

This Consumer Awareness Guide will help you navigate the "mine field' and actually turn the tables so you end up enjoying the process. And let's face it, buying a car should be an enjoyable experience. With this guide, you will discover the **Four Steps to a Hassle-Free Car Purchase**, the **Six Costly Misconceptions About Buying a Car**, the **Four Car Sales Rip-Offs to Avoid**, and the **Ten Mistakes to Avoid When Visiting a Dealership** plus much more information and insights that will put you in the "driver's seat" when it comes to buying or leasing your next car.

GORDON WRIGHT

Made in the USA
Lexington, KY
06 April 2015